PERSEPHONE

❧ HADES' TORMENT ❧

Allison Shaw

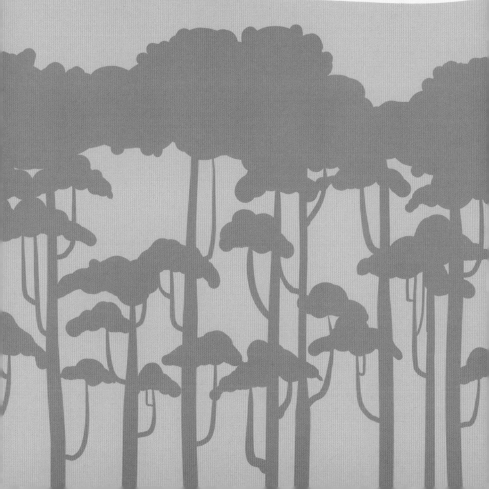

Seven Seas press and purchase enquiries can be sent to Marketing Manager
Lianne Sentar at press@gomanga.com. Information regarding the distribution
and purchase of digital editions is available from Digital Manager CK Russell
at digital@gomanga.com.

Seven Seas and the Seven Seas logo are trademarks of
Seven Seas Entertainment. All rights reserved.

Follow Seven Seas Entertainment online at
sevenseasentertainment.com.

Cover Design: Nicky Lim
Prepress Technician: Rhiannon Rasmussen-Silverstein
Production Assistant: Christa Miesner
Production Manager: Lissa Pattillo
Managing Editor: Julie Davis
Associate Publisher: Adam Arnold
Publisher: Jason DeAngelis

ISBN: 978-1-64827-651-4
Printed in China
First Printing: November 2021
10 9 8 7 6 5 4 3 2 1

CONTENTS

PERSEPHONE
HADES' TORMENT

I

BUT APOLLO, I DON'T CARE ABOUT SOME SILLY ARCHERY CONTEST!

YOU'RE JUST SCARED YOUR MOTHER WILL NOTICE YOU'RE GONE!

I'M NOT SUPPOSED TO BE SO CLOSE TO OLYMPUS!

I WAS *WONDERING* WHAT ALL THIS WAS ABOUT.

SHE DOESN'T EXACTLY LOOK HAPPY TO BE HERE...

AND THAT'S WHY I HAVE ***YOU*** HERE, EROS!
JUST ONE LITTLE STRAY ARROW FROM ***YOU*** AND SHE'LL BE PLENTY HAPPY TO BE HERE!
SHE JUST HAS TO BE LOOKING AT ME, RIGHT?

WHAT ARE THEY AIMING AT?

SURELY NOT THE BIRD?

OH NO, HOW *CARELESS* OF ME.

THESPIS WOULD BE SO PROUD.

AND NARCISSUS COULD TEACH YOU SOME SHAME.

STOP IT!
LEAVE IT BE!

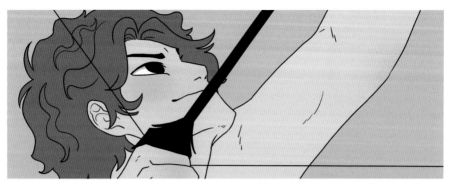

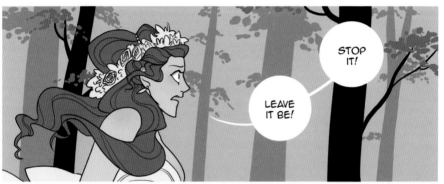

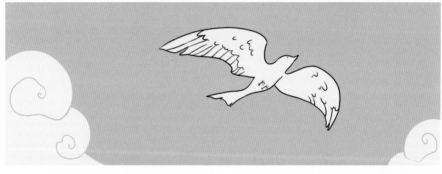

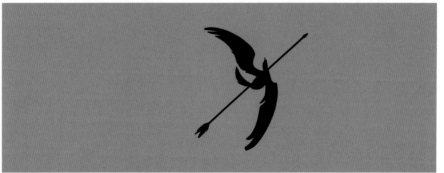

HOW COULD YOU?
YOU'RE TERRIBLE!
THE LADY HAS A POINT.
IT'S JUST A BIRD!

DID THIS BIRD *INSULT* YOU, APOLLO?
I CAN'T IMAGINE SUCH A SMALL THING WOULD BE WORTH HUNTING FOR *SPORT.*

HADES?!
OF... OF COURSE NOT!
THE BIRD JUST GOT IN THE WAY. RIGHT, ERO...
EROS?
GO HOME.
...OKAY.

EROS, YOU COWARD!
I'VE NEVER SEEN APOLLO SO... OBEDIENT.
WAIT!
PLEASE!

THE BIRD...

MAY I SEE IT?

I SUPPOSE.

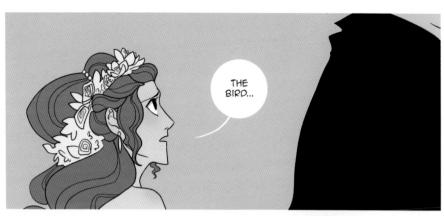

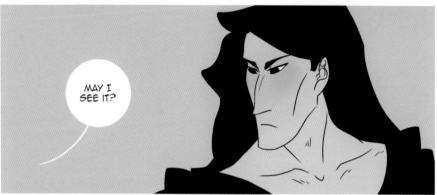

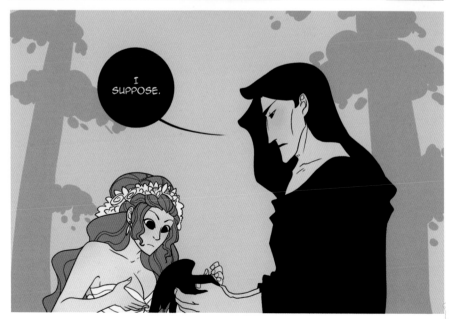

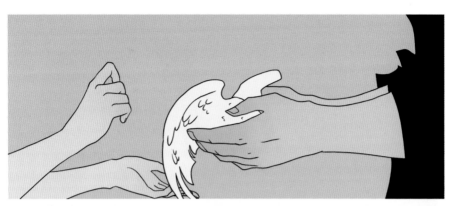

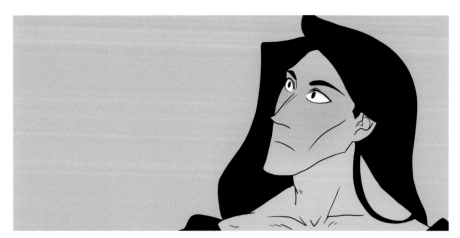

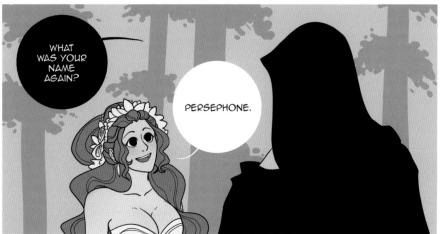

WHAT WAS YOUR NAME AGAIN?

PERSEPHONE.

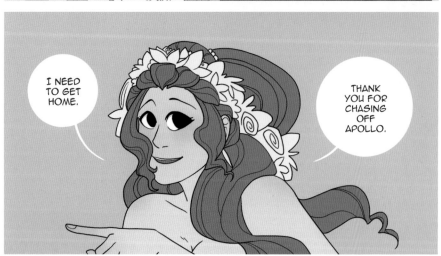

I NEED TO GET HOME.

THANK YOU FOR CHASING OFF APOLLO.

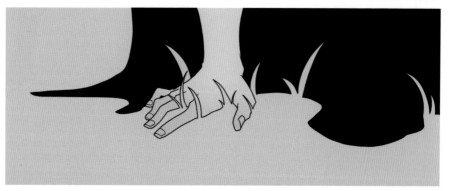

NO.
I WILL **NOT** FALL PREY TO A LESSER GOD'S MAGIC!
MASTER?

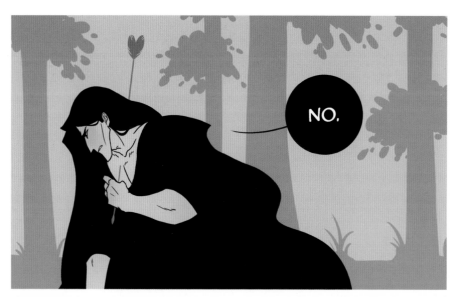

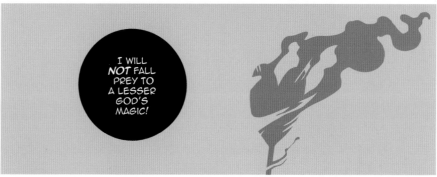

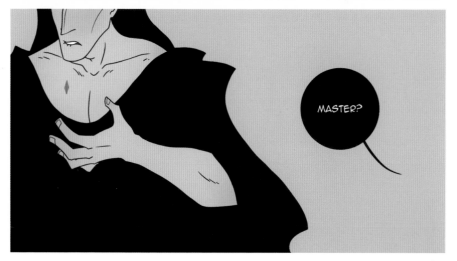

THANATOS?
PLEASE DON'T CONCERN YOURSELF WITH MY DUTIES, MASTER HADES.
APOLLO NEEDED A LESSON AND HE ISN'T SCARED OF *YOU.*

ARE YOU HARMED?
NO.
WHAT OF THE BIRD?
IT SURVIVED.
ARE YOU SURE YOU'RE UNHARMED?

I'M FINE.

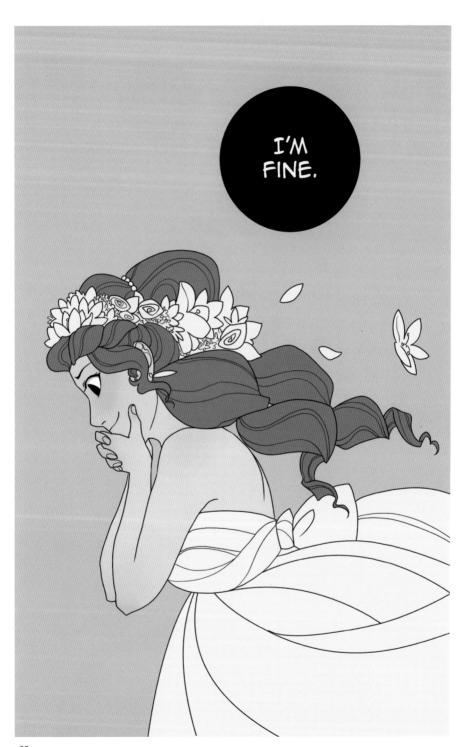

II

UM...
WHAT?

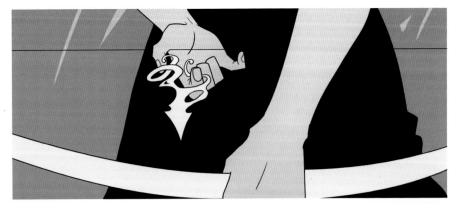

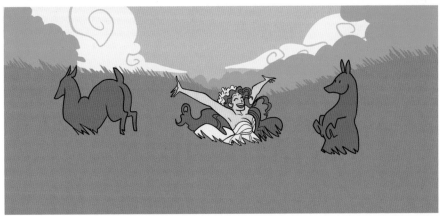

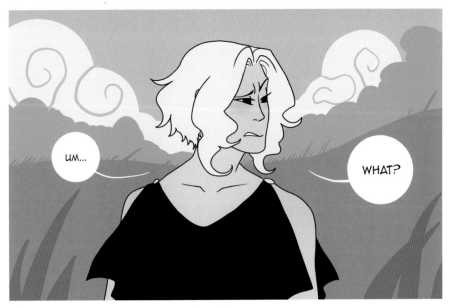

PERSEPHONE?

SO *YOU'RE* THE GIRL MY BROTHER WON'T SHUT UP ABOUT.

YOU REALLY DO LIVE OUT IN THE MIDDLE OF NOWHERE.

YOU SAY THAT LIKE IT'S A BAD THING, ARTEMIS.
DON'T YOU GET BORED OR LONELY?
I'VE GOT MY MOTHER, AND ALL THE NYMPHS ARE REALLY NICE.

BUT WHAT DO YOU EVEN DO FOR FUN OUT HERE?
YOU DON'T EXACTLY SEEM LIKE THE TYPE TO ENJOY HUNTING.
I... PICK FLOWERS?
ARE YOU SERIOUS ...?

I'M GOING TO FIX THIS.
ATALANTA'S BIG RACE IS TOMORROW AND YOU'RE GOING WITH ME!
I'LL ASK MY MOTHER, BUT I DON'T THINK SHE'D APPROVE...
I'LL MAKE SURE APOLLO STOPS BOTHERING YOU.
DEAL.

PERFECT! YOU CAN HELP ME RUB IT IN APHRODITE'S FACE WHEN ATALANTA WINS!
APHRODITE WILL BE THERE?
SHE'D BETTER BE! WE HAVE A BET GOING.
ARE...
ARE ANY OTHER GODS GOING TO BE THERE?
SOMEONE SPECIFIC IN MIND?

LIKE...
MAYBE...
HADES?
...
...WHY?
I... ENVY HIM?
NO.
I WANT TO BE LIKE HIM.

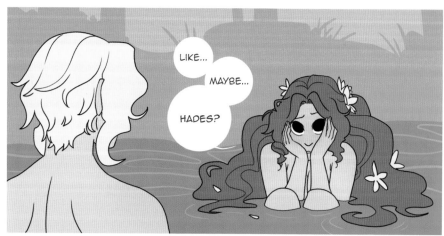

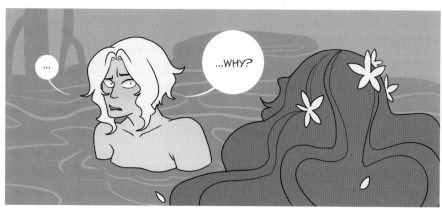

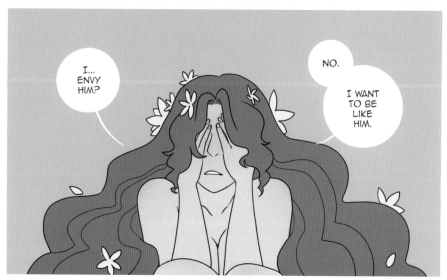

NO ONE LISTENS TO ME.
WHO CARES HOW THE HARMLESS LITTLE FLOWER GIRL FEELS?
UH...
BUT HADES HAS THIS BIG, DARK PRESENCE THAT DEMANDS RESPECT.
HE'S TERRIFYING.
I WANT TO BE JUST LIKE HIM.

HADES?
WHAT HAPPENED?
APHRODITE'S BRAT!
EVERY ARROW I PLUCK OUT IS REPLACED THREEFOLD.

MAKE HIM TAKE THEM BACK.
OR YOU COULD STOP RESISTING THEM.
IT WOULD PROBABLY DO YOU SOME GOOD.
NO.
SO, WHO'S THE LUCKY LADY?

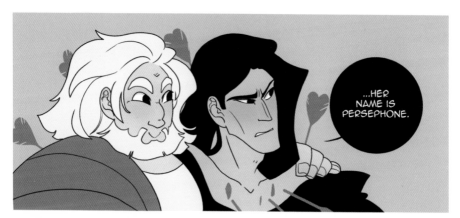

...HER NAME IS PERSEPHONE.

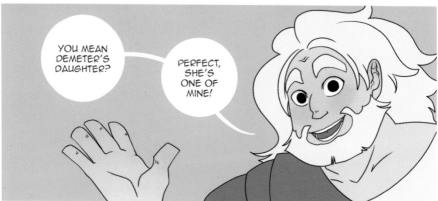

YOU MEAN DEMETER'S DAUGHTER?

PERFECT, SHE'S ONE OF MINE!

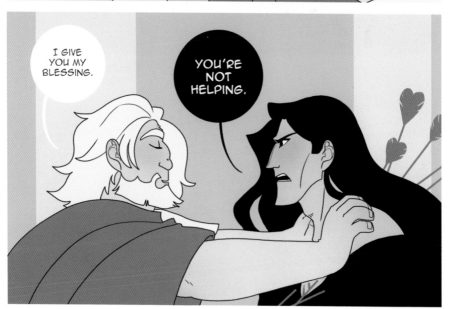

I GIVE YOU MY BLESSING.

YOU'RE NOT HELPING.

AND YOU DON'T UNDERSTAND!
SHE DESERVES ONE OF YOUR DAMNED BRIGHT-EYED OLYMPIANS!
NOT--
HADES...
NOT *THIS.*

NOT...
ME.
HADES, JUST LET ME HELP YOU--
I'LL FIND EROS MYSELF.

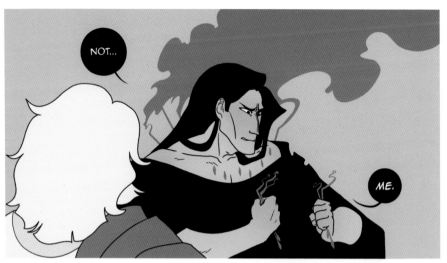

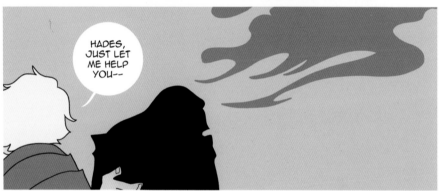

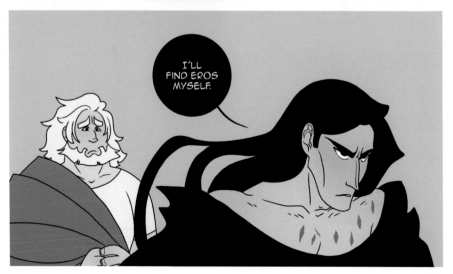

FLOWERS DON'T BLOOM IN THE DARK.

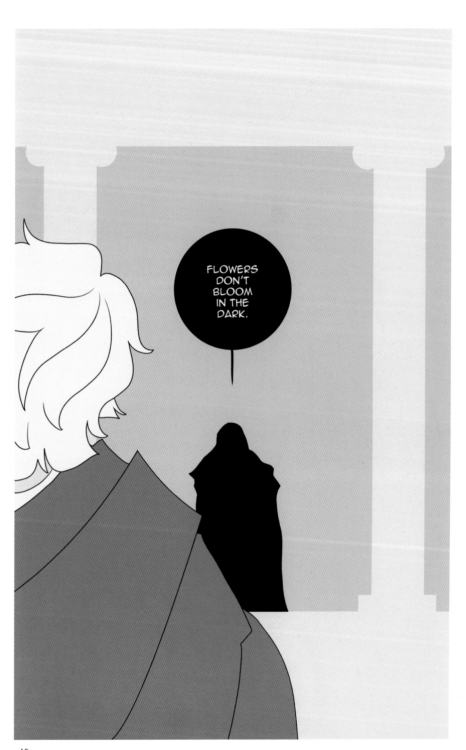

III

HOW'S THAT DUST TASTE?!

ATALANTA'S SO GREAT!
SHE WAS RAISED BY A BEAR!
WOW!
SO WHAT'S THE PRIZE FOR THIS RACE, ANYWAY?

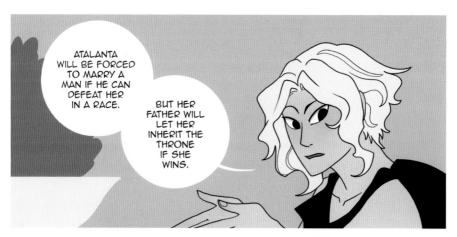

ATALANTA WILL BE FORCED TO MARRY A MAN IF HE CAN DEFEAT HER IN A RACE.

BUT HER FATHER WILL LET HER INHERIT THE THRONE IF SHE WINS.

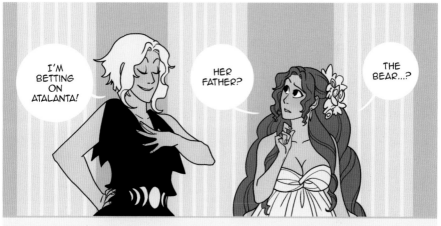

I'M BETTING ON ATALANTA!

HER FATHER?

THE BEAR...?

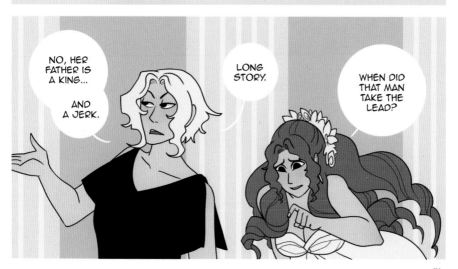

NO, HER FATHER IS A KING...

AND A JERK.

LONG STORY.

WHEN DID THAT MAN TAKE THE LEAD?

WHAT?!
WHO GAVE THAT ***STRINGBEAN*** A GOLDEN APPLE?!

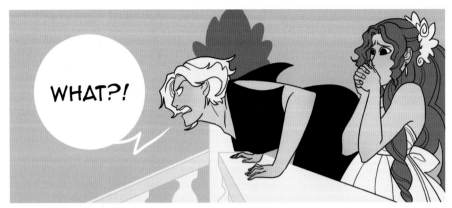

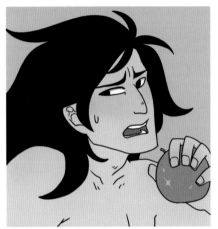

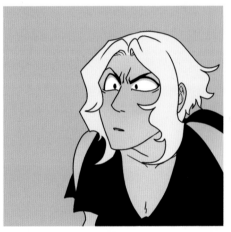

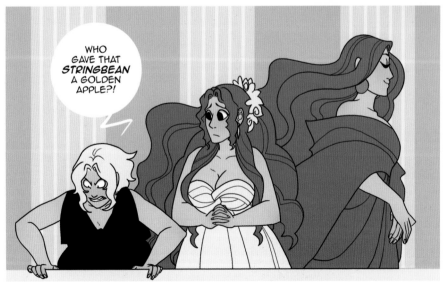

APHRODITE! YOU DIRTY CHEAT!
AND SINCE WHEN EXACTLY IS DROPPING APPLES AGAINST THE RULES OF A RACE?
I'LL SHOW YOU "AGAINST THE RULES!"
ARTEMIS, WAIT!

WELL... IT WAS FUN WHILE IT LASTED.
WHERE IS THAT LITTLE FOOL?
I KNOW HE'S--

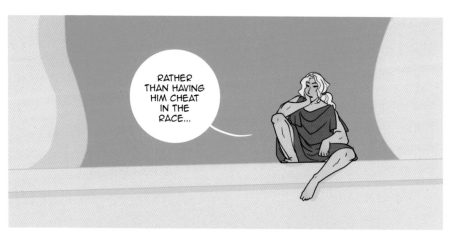

RATHER THAN HAVING HIM CHEAT IN THE RACE...

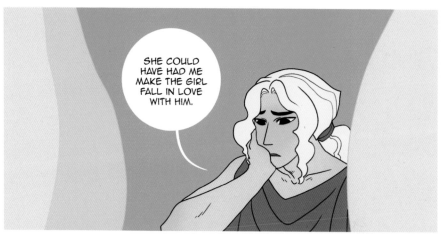

SHE COULD HAVE HAD ME MAKE THE GIRL FALL IN LOVE WITH HIM.

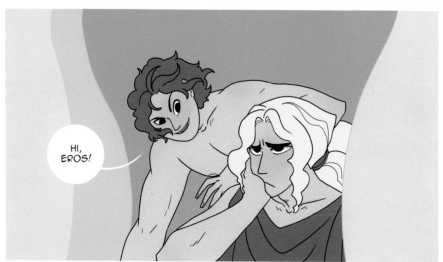

HI, EROS!

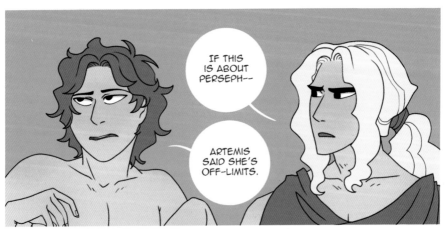

IF THIS IS ABOUT PERSEPH--

ARTEMIS SAID SHE'S OFF-LIMITS.

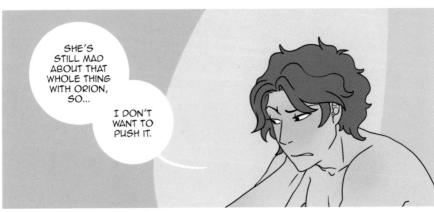

SHE'S STILL MAD ABOUT THAT WHOLE THING WITH ORION, SO...

I DON'T WANT TO PUSH IT.

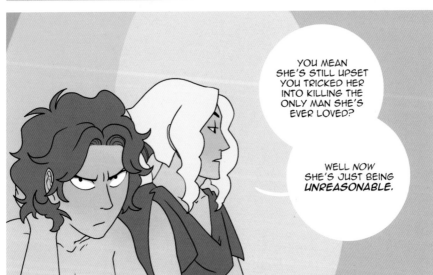

YOU MEAN SHE'S STILL UPSET YOU TRICKED HER INTO KILLING THE ONLY MAN SHE'S EVER LOVED?

WELL *NOW* SHE'S JUST BEING *UNREASONABLE.*

IF YOU'RE DONE...
I ACTUALLY NEED YOUR HELP WITH SOMETHING.
OH?
A NEW MAIDEN TO WOO?
MORE LIKE A QUESTION ABOUT HOW YOUR ARROWS WORK...
DO YOU REMEMBER PSYCHE?
THAT PRINCESS APHRODITE GOT ALL WORKED UP OVER?

I DON'T KNOW WHO YOU MADE HER FALL FOR...
BUT RUMOR HAS IT HE'S SO UGLY THAT HE WON'T EVEN SHOW HIS FACE TO HER!

HE ONLY VISITS HER IN THE DARK, YOU KNOW?
SO MY QUESTION IS...

IF I WERE TO PAY HER ONE OF SAID VISITS IN THE DARK...

WOULD SHE BE ABLE TO TELL THE DIFFERENCE?
WOULD SHE BE IN LOVE WITH ME IF SHE *THINKS* I'M HER HUSBAND?
OR DOES THE ARROW'S POWER ONLY WORK IF IT'S ACTUALLY *HIM* THERE?
AND IF I REVEALED MYSELF AS HER HUSBAND--

HOW ABOUT I SET YOU UP WITH SOMEONE EVEN PRETTIER THAN PSYCHE?
SUCH A BEAUTY EXISTS?
THERE'S ALWAYS SOMEONE PRETTIER.
AND YOU'LL HELP ME?
OF COURSE.
SHE'S IN THE CROWD DOWN THERE IF YOU WANT TO SEE.

LET'S SEE...
OH! IS IT THAT BRUNETTE?
...OR HER FRIEND?
SURE.
WHY NOT?

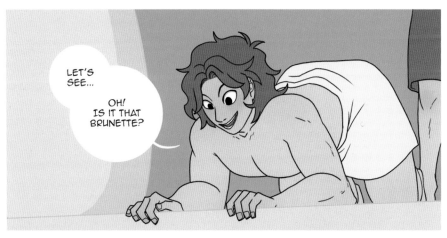

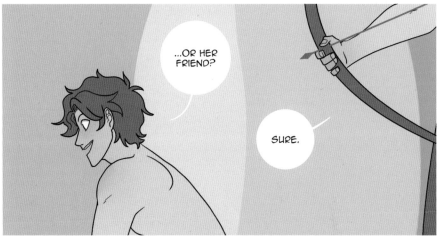

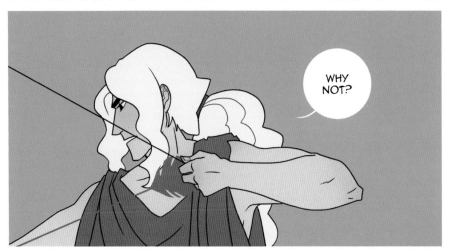

A PLEASURE TO SEE YOU AGAIN!

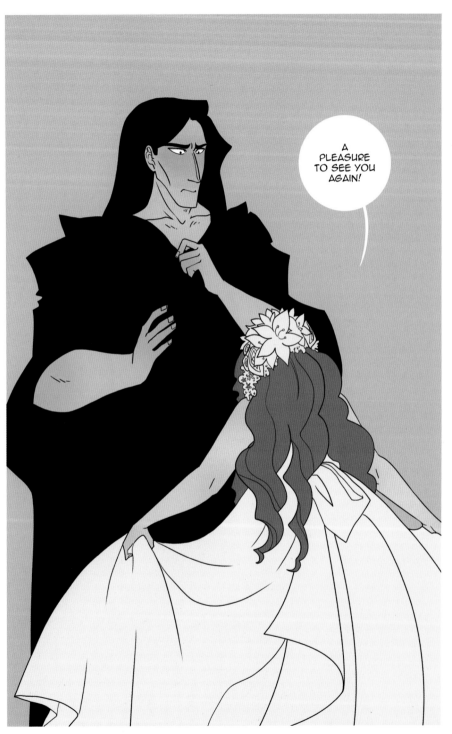

YOU MOCK ME SO OPENLY IT'S ALMOST REFRESHING.
OR ARE YOU TRULY SO PLEASED TO SEE THE KING OF THE DEAD?

IF THAT'S THE CASE, WOULD YOU CARE FOR A TOUR OF THE UNDERWORLD?
PERHAPS THAT SHOULD PLEASE YOU AS WELL?
WHAT'S IT LIKE?

...
WHAT?
THE UNDERWORLD. WHAT'S IT LIKE?
COLD.
DARK.
QUIET.
SOUNDS PEACEFUL. IS IT FAR?
THERE IS NO PLACE FURTHER.
SO THEN WE SHOULD SEE LOTS OF OTHER PLACES ALONG THE WAY.

MOTHER NEVER LETS ME GO FAR.
SHE'D BE FURIOUS IF SHE KNEW THAT I WAS HERE.

SO LET'S GO SEE THIS UNDERWORLD OF YOURS BEFORE DEAR MOTHER REALIZES I'M GONE!

ARE YOU ALWAYS SO READY TO RUN OFF WITH STRANGERS?
YOU'RE NO STRANGER, I KNOW EXACTLY WHO YOU ARE!
SOMEONE HELP!
APOLLO'S CHASING AFTER DAPHNE LIKE A STARVING BEAST!

IV

WHAT HAVE YOU DONE?!
I...

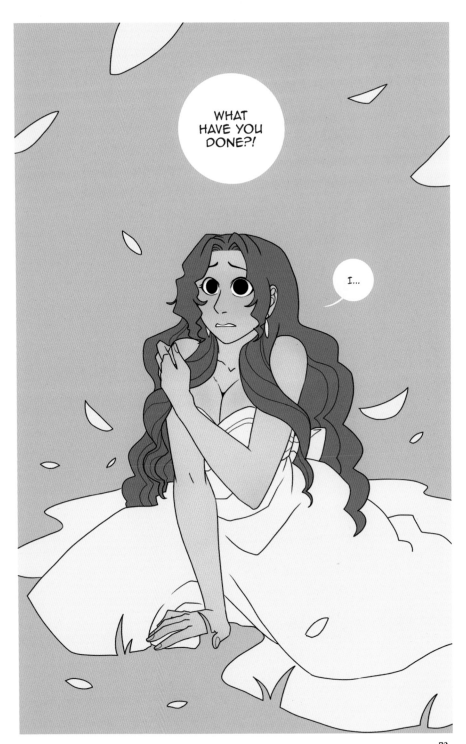

I WAS
ONLY...

TRYING
TO HELP.

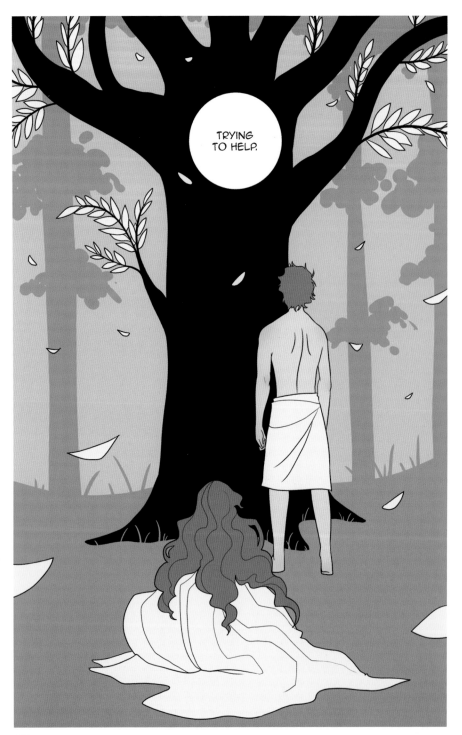

AND *THIS* IS HOW YOU *HELPED?*
BY TURNING THE POOR GIRL INTO A TREE?
I REALLY CAN'T LET YOU OUT OF MY SIGHT, CAN I?

CAN... CAN YOU UNDO IT, MOTHER?
NO, CHILD.
IT'S LIKELY FOR THE BEST. I HEARD APOLLO WAS SHOT BY EROS.
HIS MOTHER REALLY NEEDS TO REIN HIM IN, WITH MAGIC THAT POTENT.
OH, STOP. THERE ARE WORSE WAYS THIS COULD HAVE ENDED.
AND AT LEAST HE WASN'T CHASING *YOU.*

WHAT WOULD YOU HAVE DONE *THEN?*

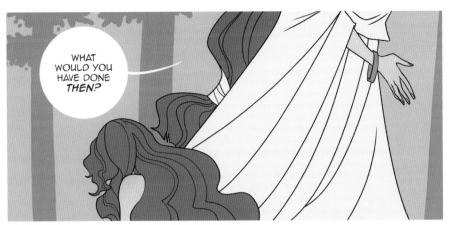

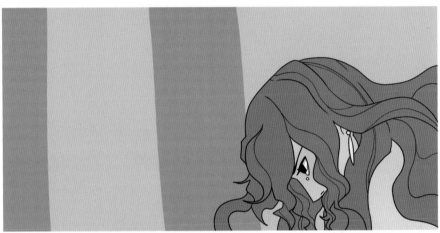

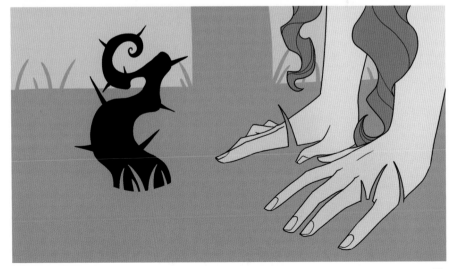

LET'S GO HOME WHERE YOU'RE SAFE.

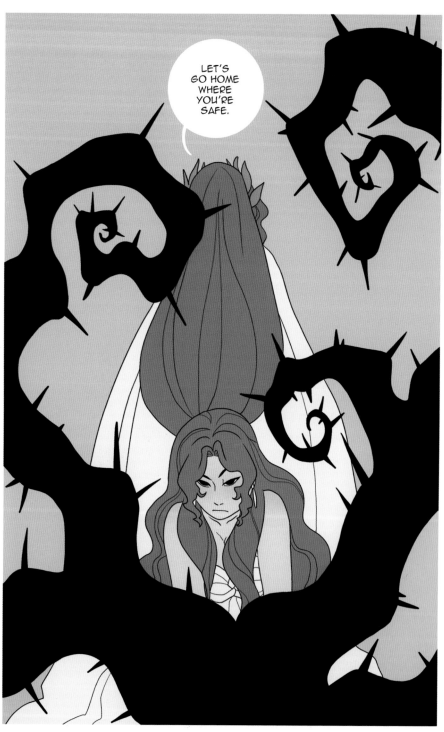

YES, MOTHER.

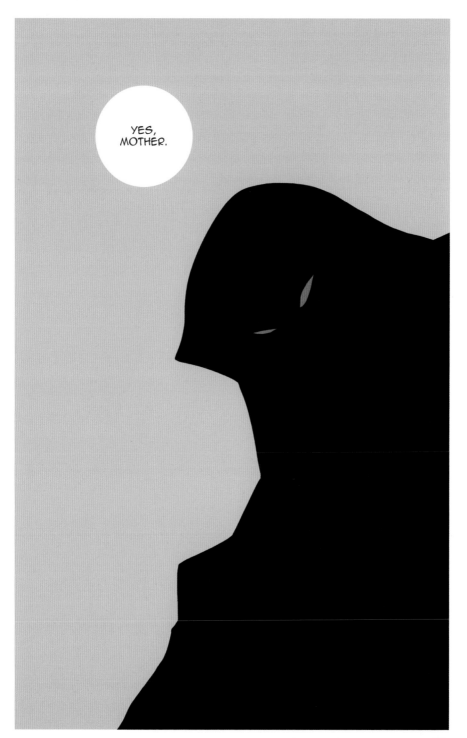

EXPLAIN YOURSELF.

I COULDN'T HELP IT!
EROS SHOT ME AND I--

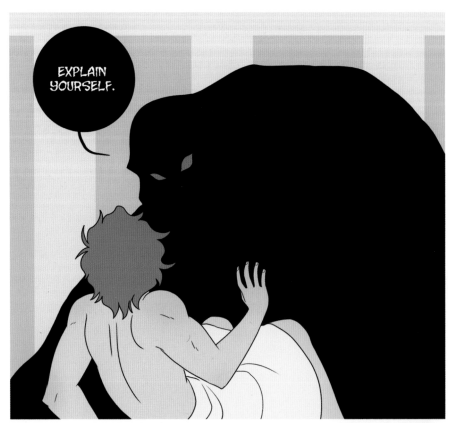

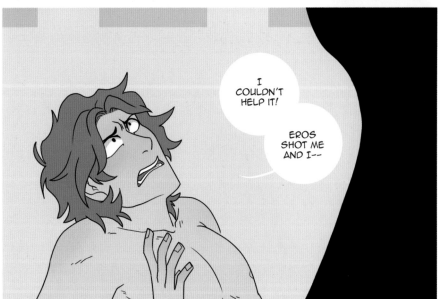

IS THAT YOUR EXCUSE?
A LONE ARROW ABSOLVES YOU OF ALL RESPONSIBILITY FOR YOUR ACTIONS?
THAT'S EASY FOR YOU TO SAY!

YOU'VE...
NEVER...
BEEN...
SHOT.

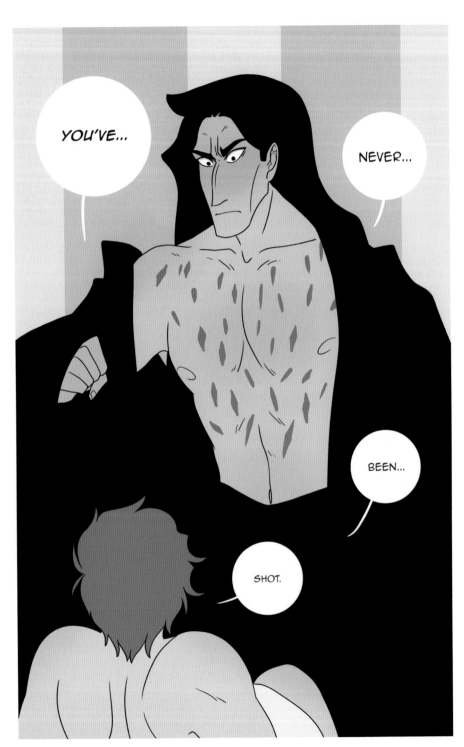

SELFISH PEOPLE LIKE YOU AND YOUR FATHER LEAVE THE LIVING WORLD AN ABSOLUTE MESS.
WHO DO YOU THINK IS FORCED TO DEAL WITH THE AFTERMATH IN THE UNDERWORLD?
I CAN'T GIVE EVERYONE JUSTICE.
LEAST OF ALL THOSE WRONGED BY A GOD.

SHOULD I EVER CATCH YOU IN MY REALM...
I SHALL SHOW YOU A MOST APPROPRIATE ETERNITY.
THEN AGAIN, PERHAPS THERE IS SOMEONE ELSE WHO CAN SAVE ME THE TROUBLE...

AND I DON'T THINK YOUR IMMORTALITY WOULD SPARE YOU FROM HER MAGIC THE WAY IT DOES FROM MINE.

V

I JUST WANTED TO DISTRACT HIM.
I DIDN'T THINK HE'D ATTACK HER LIKE THAT.

HE WAS SCHEMING AFTER THE ONE PERSON I ACTUALLY CARE ABOUT.
SHE'S SO WITTY AND PERFECT BUT ALL APOLLO CAN SEE IS ANOTHER CUTE FACE.

AND I... DON'T WANT HER TO KNOW WHO I AM.
SHE ***CAN'T*** KNOW.

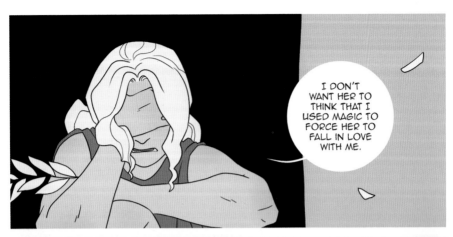

I DON'T WANT HER TO THINK THAT I USED MAGIC TO FORCE HER TO FALL IN LOVE WITH ME.

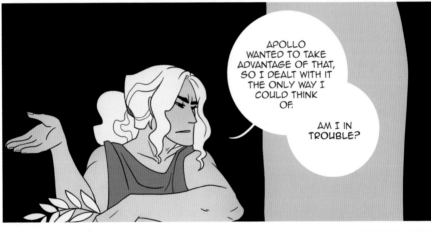

APOLLO WANTED TO TAKE ADVANTAGE OF THAT, SO I DEALT WITH IT THE ONLY WAY I COULD THINK OF.

AM I IN TROUBLE?

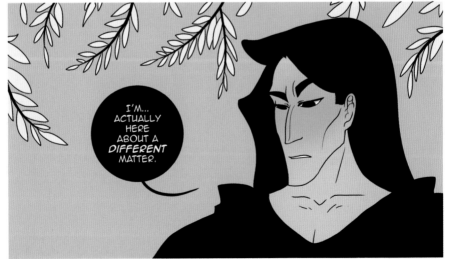

I'M... ACTUALLY HERE ABOUT A *DIFFERENT* MATTER.

...HUH.
FIX IT.
WHY? SHE SUITS YOU BETTER THAN YOU THINK.
I SINCERELY DOUBT THAT. *FIX IT.*
IF YOU *INSIST.*
ONE SCRATCH FROM THIS AND YOU'LL GO BACK TO FEELING NOTHING.

NOTHING AT ALL?
NOT A THING.
YOU'RE A STRONGER MAN THAN I AM.
I SCRATCHED MYSELF WITH AN ARROW MEANT FOR PSYCHE BY ACCIDENT.
I KNEW EXACTLY HOW TO REVERSE IT.
I JUST COULDN'T DO IT.
I LIKE THE ACHE.

SHE IS LIKE AIR TO ME.
HOW CAN I GO BACK TO HOLDING MY BREATH?
I NEVER EXPECTED ANYONE WOULD DENY MY ARROW, SINCE IN MY MIND THAT WOULD BE LIKE REFUSING TO BREATHE.
I'M SORRY FOR ALL THE ANGUISH I'VE CAUSED YOU.
OH AND BY THE WAY, FOR THAT ARROW TO WORK...
YOU NEED TO BE ***LOOKING*** AT HER.

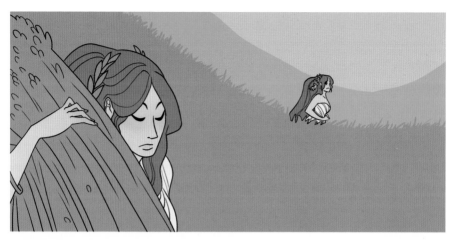

AND JUST **WHERE** DO YOU THINK YOU'RE GOING?

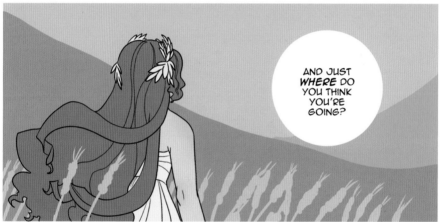

JUST... PICKING FLOWERS.

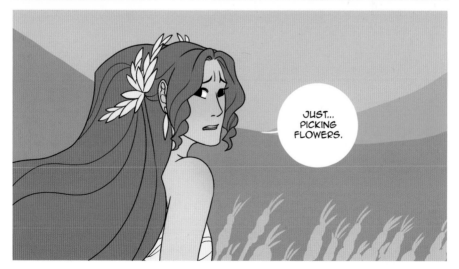

RIGHT, LIKE HOW YOU WERE "PICKING FLOWERS" WHEN YOU GOT MIXED UP WITH APOLLO?
BUT MOTHER--
I DON'T THINK SO.
YOU'RE STAYING HERE.
HAVE YOU LEARNED NOTHING?
YOU HAVE SEEN FIRSTHAND WHAT THEY DO TO THOSE WHO CAN'T STOP THEM.
THIS IS WHERE YOU ARE SAFE!

YOU WILL STAY WHERE I CAN SEE YOU BECAUSE I CAN'T TRUST YOU TO UNDERSTAND THAT!
I'M NOT A CHILD!
YES, YOU ARE!
ONLY CHILDREN DISOBEY THEIR PARENTS!
NOW--
WHAT?!

PERSEPHONE!

WAIT!

PERSEPHONE!

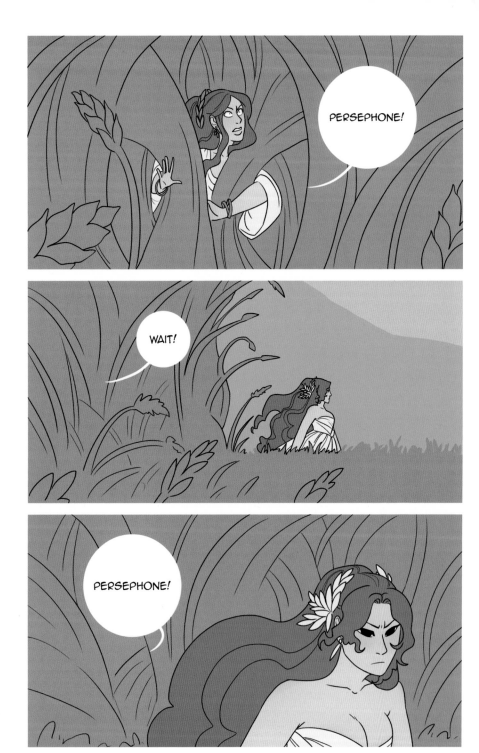

OH NO...

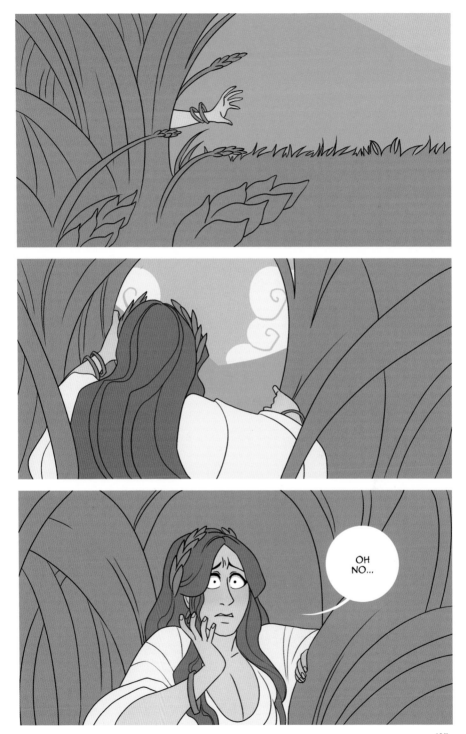

AH!

HM?

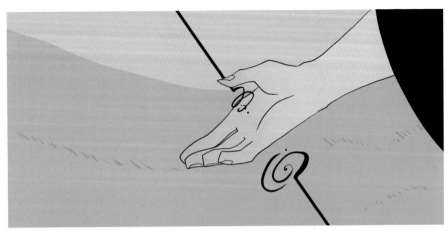

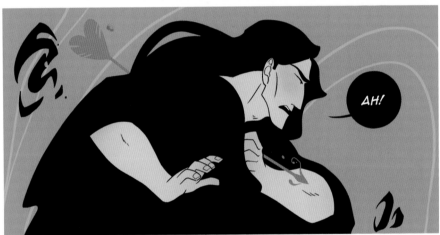

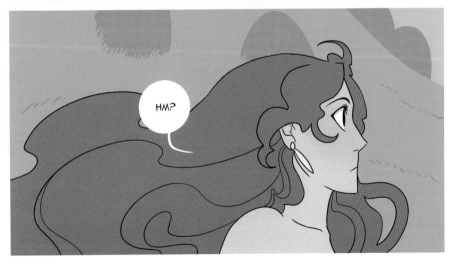

WELL...
NO ONE TO BLAME BUT MYSELF, NOW.

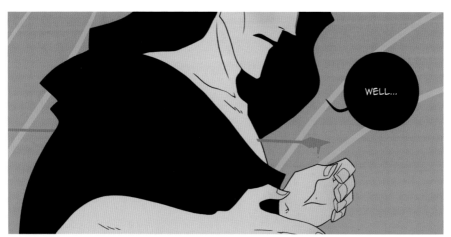

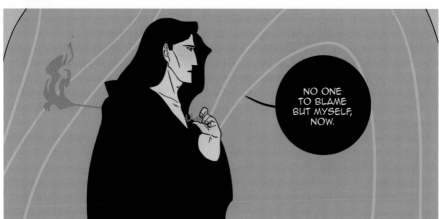

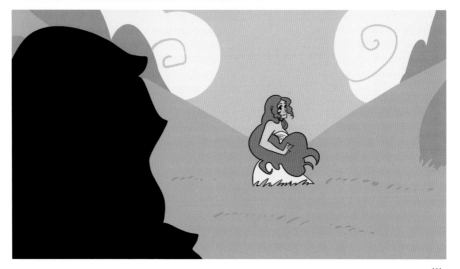

HADES?

WHAT ARE YOU DOING SO FAR OUT HERE?

HELLO, PERSEPHONE.

IT SOUNDED LIKE YOU WERE IN PAIN JUST NOW.

ARE YOU HURT?

IT WAS NOTHING.
I MERELY--

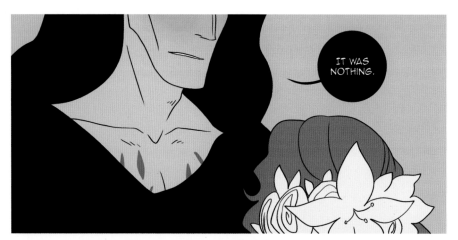

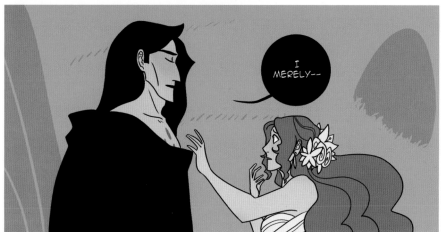

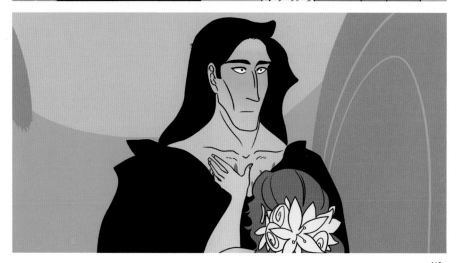

VI

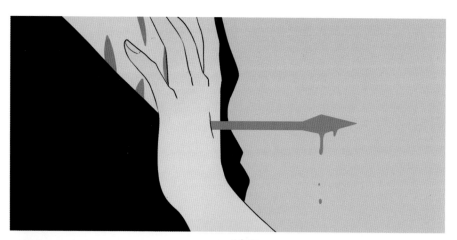

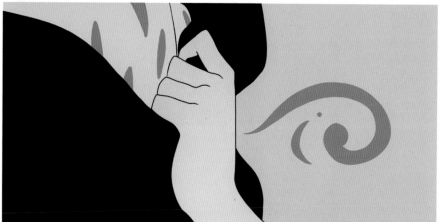

PERSEPHONE, PLEASE--

IF YOU GIVE INTO IT SO EASILY--
I WON'T BE ABLE TO...
HADES...
AM I... **BOTHERING** YOU?

NO.
BECAUSE, IF I AM--

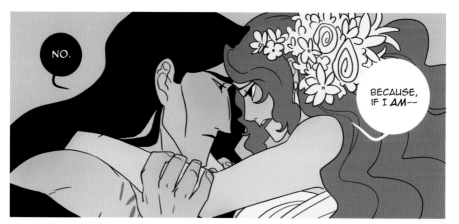

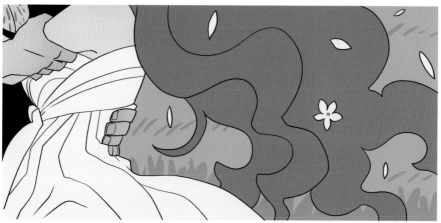

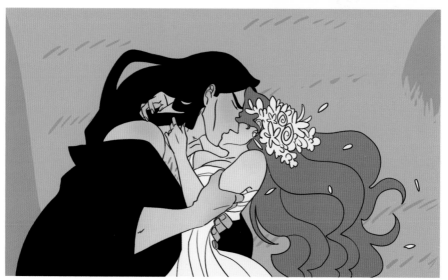

SO, UM...
ABOUT THAT TOUR YOU PROMISED ME...

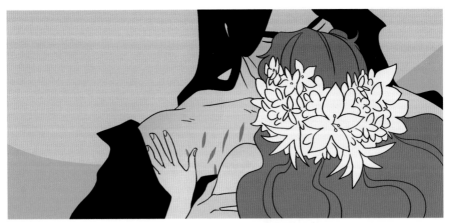

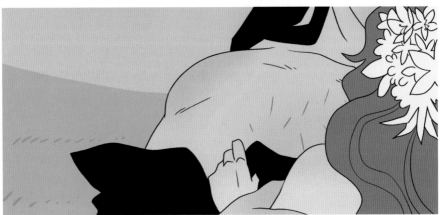

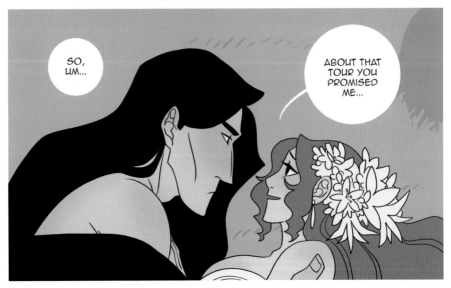

COULD YOU...
TAKE ME NOW?
I'M GOING TO ASSUME THAT WAS ON PURPOSE.

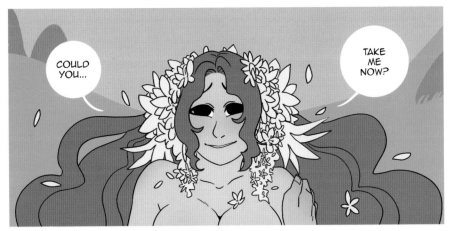

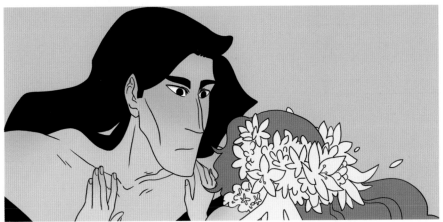

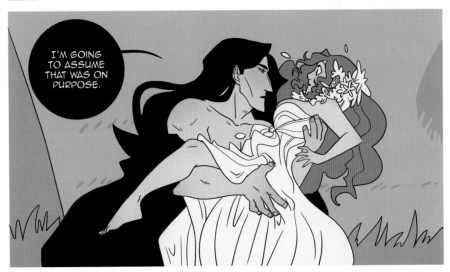

AH!

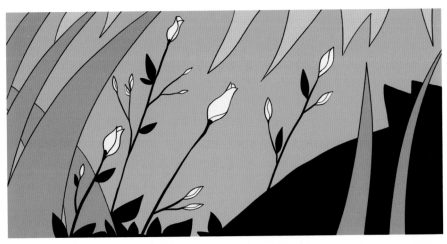

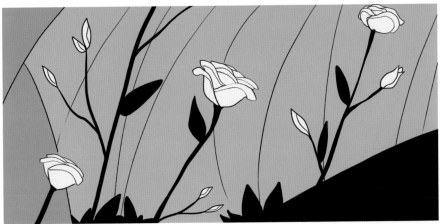

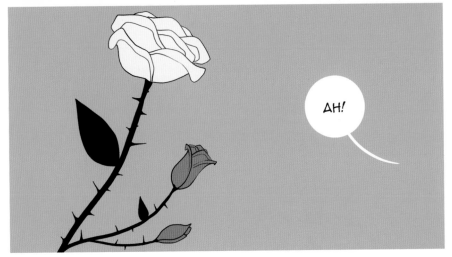

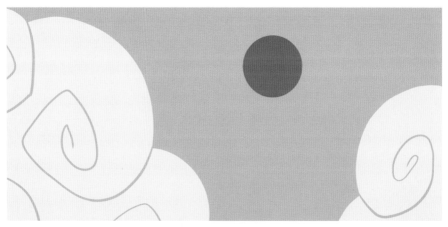

PERSEPHONE!

125

WHAT IS ALL THIS?

DID SHE MAKE THESE?

SUCH AN ANGRY-LOOKING FLOWER...

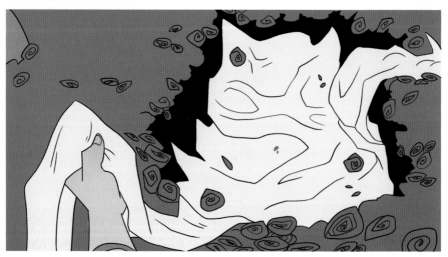

I THOUGHT YOU SAID THIS PLACE WAS COLD?
WELL...
IT WAS.

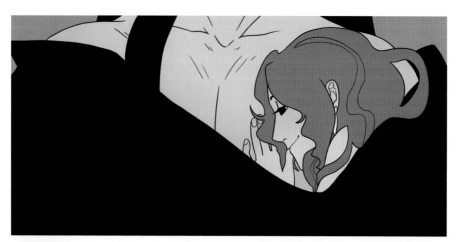

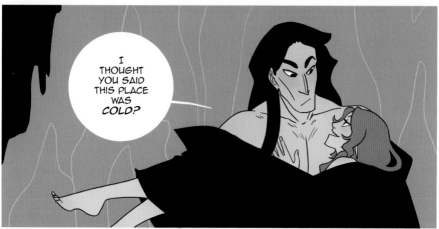

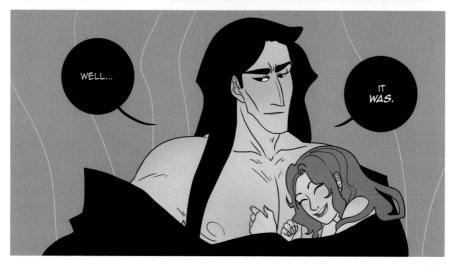

VII

THOUGHT YOU COULD SMUGGLE HER AWAY SO EASILY, DID YOU?
SHE MAY HAVE TURNED ME AWAY *BEFORE...*
BUT AFTER THIS, I'LL BE HER HERO!
SORRY, HADES-- BUT YOU REALLY SHOULD'VE PICKED A DIFFERENT GIRL TO STEAL.

FEAR NOT, FAIR PERSEPHONE!
OH FOR CRYING OUT LOUD...

FOR I HAVE COME TO RESCUE YOU!
HERMES? WHO LET YOU IN?

YOU'VE CROSSED THE LINE THIS TIME, HADES!
ZEUS DEMANDS PERSEPHONE BE RETURNED TO HER MOTHER IMMEDIATELY!
...
NO.
LET ME REPHRASE THAT--
ZEUS *ORDERS* YOU TO--
HE HAS *HIS* REALM, I HAVE *MINE.*

YOU CAN'T JUST IGNORE ORDERS FROM ZEUS!
YOU MIGHT BE KING DOWN HERE, BUT SHE BELONGS IN THE REALM OF THE LIVING!
HADES!

HERMES IS REALLY PERSISTENT, BUT HE'S ALSO KIND OF AN IDIOT.
IT'LL BE EASIER TO TRICK HIM INTO LEAVING THAN JUST TELLING HIM "NO."

YOU KNOW THIS FROM EXPERIENCE?
APOLLO WASN'T THE ONLY ONE WHO WOULDN'T TAKE NO FOR AN ANSWER.
IN FACT, I THINK YOU'RE THE ONLY ONE WHO EVER TOOK MY FEELINGS INTO CONSIDERATION.

HERMES, MAY I SPEAK TO YOU FOR A MOMENT?
...
BUT THAT SOUNDS COMPLETELY RIDICULOUS!

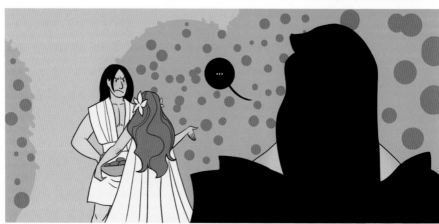

I'M... I'M NOT HUNGRY!
PROVE ME WRONG, THEN.
IT ONLY TOOK A SINGLE BITE FOR *ME.*
I'M GOING TO PASS THIS ON TO ZEUS AND SEE IF THERE IS A CURE!

DON'T WORRY, PERSEPHONE! I'LL BE BACK FOR YOU SOON!
UNTIL THEN!
WHAT DID YOU TELL HIM?
OH, NOTHING TERRIBLY CLEVER.

SEEDS.
SHE IS BOUND TO THE UNDERWORLD BECAUSE OF... *POMEGRANATE* *SEEDS.*
THAT'S WHAT SHE SAID, YES.
THAT'S JUST WHAT I GET FOR SENDING ***YOU,*** I SUPPOSE.

HA HA HA HA HA
AHA HA HA HA HEE HEE
HA HA
DID HE ACTUALLY *BELIEVE* THAT?
WELL, HE REFUSED TO *TEST* IT!

OH... THEY LOOK SO HAPPY TOGETHER.
YOU COULD LEAVE THEM BE, YOU KNOW.
EVEN IF ALL THE MORTALS WERE TO STARVE, I WOULD JUST BRING THEM HERE.
THE UNDERWORLD ISN'T SO BAD NOW THAT MISS PERSEPHONE IS HERE.
AND MASTER HADES IS A FINE RULER, THEY'LL SEE!

OH, BUT THANATOS... THEY WOULD SUFFER SO MUCH.
NEITHER OF THOSE TWO WOULD WANT THAT.
AND IT'S NOT FAIR TO KEEP LETTING DEMETER THINK HER DAUGHTER IS IN DANGER.
HOPEFULLY SHE'LL BE MORE REASONABLE ONCE SHE SEES THE GIRL IS FINE.
AS LONG AS DEMETER IS DOING HER JOB, I DON'T SEE ANY REASON WHY THOSE TWO SHOULD HAVE TO BE SEPARATED.

BESIDES, THAT POOR GIRL HAS SPENT HER WHOLE LIFE BEING HIDDEN AWAY FROM EVERYONE.
IT'S ABOUT TIME SHE PROPERLY INTRODUCES HERSELF, ISN'T IT?
LADY HEKATE...
I DO NOT WANT MY MASTER TO SUFFER ALONE.
CAN YOU PROMISE ME...?

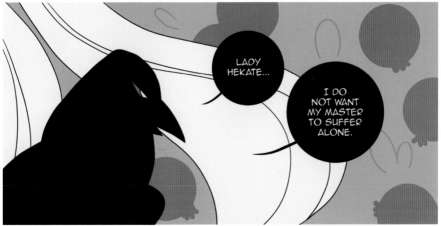

A PROMISE, THEN.

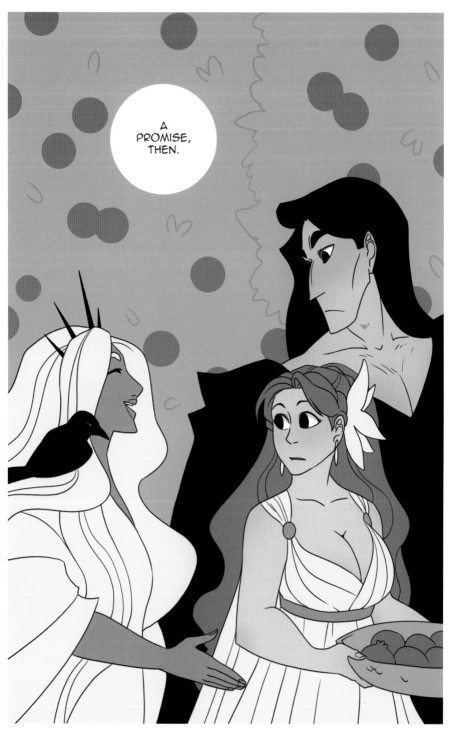

VIII

THANATOS!

HELLO, MYNTHE.

IS HADES NEARBY?
I HAVEN'T SEEN HIM IN AGES!

HE HAD SO MANY STRANGE WOUNDS THE LAST TIME I SAW HIM... EVEN *MY* WATERS COULDN'T HEAL THEM!
OH, THAT WAS JUST BECAUSE OF PERSEPHONE. DON'T WORRY ABOUT IT.

"PERSEPHONE"? WHO IS THAT?
YOU'LL SEE IN A MOMENT.

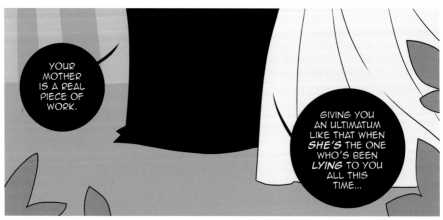

YOUR MOTHER IS A REAL PIECE OF WORK.

GIVING YOU AN ULTIMATUM LIKE THAT WHEN *SHE'S* THE ONE WHO'S BEEN *LYING* TO YOU ALL THIS TIME...

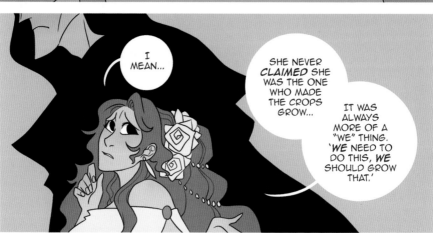

I MEAN...

SHE NEVER *CLAIMED* SHE WAS THE ONE WHO MADE THE CROPS GROW...

IT WAS ALWAYS MORE OF A "WE" THING. '*WE* NEED TO DO THIS, *WE* SHOULD GROW THAT.'

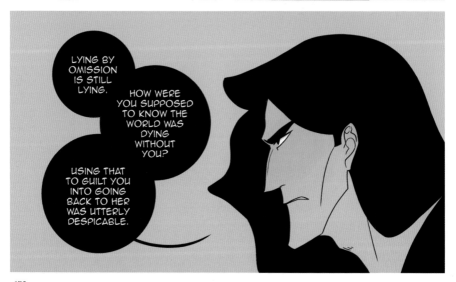

LYING BY OMISSION IS STILL LYING.

HOW WERE YOU SUPPOSED TO KNOW THE WORLD WAS DYING WITHOUT YOU?

USING THAT TO GUILT YOU INTO GOING BACK TO HER WAS UTTERLY DESPICABLE.

THANK GOODNESS FOR LADY HEKATE'S QUICK THINKING, AT LEAST!
IT NEVER WOULD HAVE OCCURRED TO ME TO REARRANGE THE GROWING CYCLES TO FIT INTO HALF THE YEAR!
I CERTAINLY DON'T *WANT* TO SPEND HALF THE YEAR APART, BUT...
IT'S BETTER THAN THE *WHOLE* YEAR.
YES.

THAT'S HER?
YES.
I DON'T GET IT!
WHY ARE THEY SO CHUMMY?
WELL, THEY *ARE* MARRIED, AFTER ALL.

HM?
WHAT?!
I THOUGHT YOU SAID SHE WAS THE ONE WHO WOUNDED HADES!
WHY WOULD HE MARRY THE ONE WHO CAUSED HIM SO MUCH SUFFERING?!
MYNTHE?

YOU DON'T NEED TO BE SHY.
UH...
HI.
THIS IS MYNTHE, THE NYMPH OF THIS SPRING.
HELLO!

MYNTHE, THIS IS PERSEPHONE.
N... NICE TO MEET YOU.
OH NO, SHE'S CUTE!
YOUR SPRING IS LOVELY!
IT HAS A WONDERFUL SCENT AND THE TEMPERATURE IS PERFECT!
...

OH NO, SHE'S NICE!
YES, WELL...
THIS WATER ALSO HAS HEALING PROPERTIES.
NOT THAT IT DID ANY GOOD ON THOSE WOUNDS OF YOURS FROM LAST TIME, HUH, HADES?

WELL...
I'D SAY IT ALL WORKED OUT.
OH NO, THEY'RE REALLY HOT TOGETHER!!
EH... WHAT?

THOSE WOUNDS WERE FROM EROS' ARROW.
THEY GOT WORSE WHEN I TRIED TO FIGHT THEIR POWER.
I WAS JUST TOO EMBARRASSED TO EXPLAIN BEFORE.
OH!
I... I SEE!
THAT'D CERTAINLY EXPLAIN THE GRABBING.
WHY DIDN'T THAT STUPID BIRD SAY SO FROM THE START?!
IS IT MAKING YOU UNCOMFORTABLE, MYNTHE?
I'M SORRY, IT'S HARD TO STOP--
I NEVER SAID THAT.

IN FACT...

MIND IF I GIVE HER A PROPER WELCOME?

HM... THOSE ARE NEW.

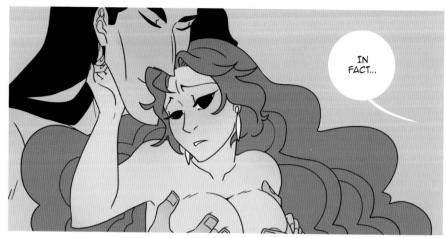

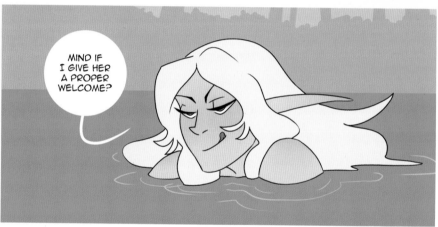

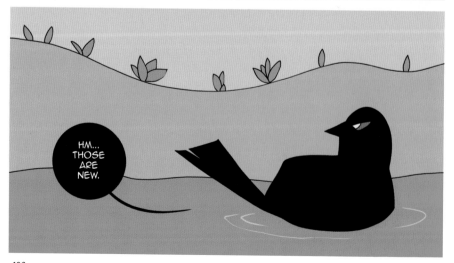

163

SO SHE MAKES PLANTS GROW WHEN SHE'S HAPPY?
SHE'S SO SWEET! MAKE SURE HADES KNOWS SHE'S WELCOME ANYTIME.

I'VE NEVER SEEN HADES SO HAPPY.
IT'S A NICE CHANGE.
YES.

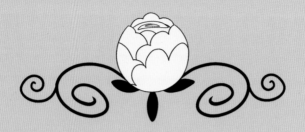

About the Creator

Allison Shaw is a self-taught artist from Jacksonville, Florida. During a period of unemployment in 2016, she began crafting a feel-good, romantic comic published in monthly installments online for paying subscribers, while keeping up with her regular webcomics *Tigress Queen* and *Far to the North*. Spinning Greek myths into a feminist romance turned out to be one of the best decisions she'd ever made. She never could have dreamed that Persephone would gather so much attention and is very grateful to her loving spouse, supportive mother, and the lovely people who supported the book that first allowed her to make comics her full-time career.

Social: twitter.com/AlliDrawsComics